CONTENT ANALYSIS: HOW AND WHY?

By

N. Jayapriya M.Sc., M.Ed., NET (Edn)

SHANLAX PUBLICATIONS

Madurai, Tamil Nadu, India

CONTENT ANALYSIS: HOW AND WHY?

First Edition: 2018

ISBN: 978-93-87102-90-3

Publisher
SHANLAX PUBLICATIONS
61, 66 T.P.K. Main Road
Vasantha Nagar
Madurai – 625003
Tamil Nadu, India

Ph: 0452-4208765,
Mobile: 7639303383
email:publisher@shanlaxpublications.com
web: www.shanlaxpublications.com

Dedicated to
My Inspiring Mother

Prof. V. Renuga Devi
Emeritus Professor
Former Chairperson
School of Linguistics and Communication
Former Head, Dept. of Linguistics
Madurai Kamaraj University

Foreword

Textbooks are the resourceful and systemized units of work. Even in this digital era, textbooks are the essential tool for the teachers and students for making effective teaching/learning process. Generally, a textbook covers all the units of the syllabus of that particular discipline. Textbooks are a comprehensive series of teaching procedures that inform the teachers what to do and when to do it. Textbooks offer both administrators of the educational institutions and the teachers with an inclusive and full-fledged teaching/learning program. Usually, textbooks are formulated according to the learning needs and the grasping capacity of the children at the particular age group. The National Policy on Education was implemented in 1986; and in 1988 the National Curriculum for Elementary and Secondary Education was enacted. It recommended 12 years of school education which should be child-centered and suggested a reorganization of curricular and instructional materials. It also advised to bring out examination reforms and the execution of Continuous and Comprehensive Evaluation at all stages of education. The National Curriculum Framework (2005) recommended for connecting knowledge to life outside school and for enriching the curriculum for overall development of children; so that it goes beyond textbooks. For all these reasons, the textbooks are to be framed very carefully and without any flaws. Good textbooks which are designed carefully are wonderful teaching aids.

Ms. Jayapriya is a sincere teacher educator and has flair of research. Her enthusiastic participation in the organization of seminar, conferences and workshops show her interest and talent in the educational endeavours. She published many research articles in renowned journals. She had submitted her Ph.D. thesis and will be awarded the doctoral degree shortly.

In her book entitled, “Content Analysis: How and Why?” Ms. Jayapriya explored the contents of the 10th Science textbook elaborately and put forth the positive and negative points of this textbook. Through Content Analysis research method, we can specify the relevant features of the textbook like the purpose of the textbook, coverage of syllabus, prejudices, and misunderstanding of the makers of the textbooks. Ms. Jayapriya did a thorough research of the contents of the book and has pointed out the merits and demerits of the contents included in each unit (totally, there are 8 units). She had investigated the appropriateness of the contents, the themes of the contents, the spelling mistakes and the various spellings for the same content (for example, Bactria), the merits like modernity of the illustration and defects like non-labeling in the illustrations given in the textbook.

Today’s children are called “digital natives’ and even though digitally manipulated, the children depend on textbooks which act as a tool for their education. All the school and higher education teachers depend on textbooks. Textbooks decide the classroom activities also. Teachers are the persons to decide which textbook is suitable to fulfill the aim of making awareness about the particular discipline among the students and to help the teachers and students to identify the competencies of the students. The findings and recommendation of the study made by Ms. Jayapriya will be very useful to the textbook developers. The textbook makers are responsible to take the required actions to ‘ensure the quality of science education for making the learner a scientifically literate person’ as she mentioned in her book.

I wish Ms. Jayapriya to write many books and bless her to get a successful academic career.

Dr. K. PASUMPON
Deputy Director,
Dept. of Tamil Development, Madurai

CONTENT

INTRODUCTION

The success of an educational system revolves around the effectiveness of teachers. "An effective teacher may be understood as one who helps the development of basic skills, understanding, proper work habits, desirable attitudes, value judgments and adequate personal adjustment of the teachers".

In today's classrooms, textbooks serve as tool and tutor, guidebook and gauge. Teachers throughout the world use texts to guide their instruction, so textbooks greatly influence how content is delivered (Association for Supervision and Curriculum Development, 1997). Schmidt, McKnight, and Raizen (1997) identified textbooks are playing an important role in making the leap from intentions and plans to classroom activities, by making content available, organizing it, and setting out learning tasks in a form designed to be appealing to students.

To make the most effective use of a textbook, however, teachers must decide which textbooks are appropriate for their needs. A teacher needs to determine the extent to which a textbook focuses on and is aligned with a coherent set of significant, age-appropriate student learning goals that the teacher, school, or district has identified as integral to the understanding of and progress in a particular academic subject. They must also assess how well a textbook's instructional design effectively supports the attainment of those specified learning goals. The only way to gain this information is through careful evaluations of textbooks and other curriculum materials.

A textbook is a manual of instruction or a standard book in any branch of study. It is the general and major instructional material of the teaching-learning process. It serves as an important segment of the teaching-learning process.

Textbooks are probably the most frequently used instructional material in different levels of education. They communicate the course content to the teacher and the learner, and become an important source in progressing toward the objectives of the course. In fact, in many elementary and secondary schools, a large part of the knowledge to which students are exposed comes from the textbook.

Textbooks provide some degree of content expertise for subject matter issues, a logical sequence of content and a variety of support activities like questions, test items, cases and summaries. They may help make the teaching content-oriented and comprehensive, and allow more effective use of teacher time. However, in many educational systems textbooks have a controlling impact on what is taught in schools. Some researchers even argue that textbooks tend to be the primary influence on classroom instruction.

Content analysis or textual analysis is a methodology in the social sciences for studying the content of the communication. Earl Babbie defines it as "the study of recorded human communications, such as books, websites, paintings and laws."

Due to the fact that it can be applied to examine any piece of writing or occurrence of recorded communication, content analysis is used in a large number of fields, ranging from marketing and media studies, to literature and rhetoric, ethnography and cultural studies, gender and age issues, sociology and political science, psychology and cognitive science, as well as other fields of inquiry. Additionally, content analysis reflects a close relationship with socio- and psycholinguistics, and is playing an integral role in the development of artificial intelligence.

There are two general categories of content analysis: conceptual analysis and relational analysis. Conceptual analysis can be thought of as establishing the existence and frequency of concepts in a text. Relational analysis builds on conceptual analysis by examining the relationships among concepts in a text.

The major aim of education was the acquisition of a fund of information not many years back. So curriculum was considered synonymous with subject of instruction. But now education is regarded as a dynamic process and so the aims and objectives have changed. It is not merely the course of study but the sum total of the experiences the students receive through the manifold activities that go on in the school, in the classroom, in the laboratory, in the workshop, in the playground and in the numerous informal contacts between the teacher and the students. It is much more than mere subject matter as it is traditionally conceived. In other words, the whole life in the school constitutes curriculum. Science curriculum is a part of the whole curriculum and plays an important role in the development of balanced personality of the student.

Effective learning requires systematic organization of subject matter. The type of organization determines whether the principles and concepts should be learnt by application. After selecting the subject matter based on the objectives of teaching science and the levels of students, it should be organized in a manner that influences the teaching of the subject. The content of the textbook should serve the purpose and aims of teaching. The content should be organized in accordance with the principle of psychology and it should arrange systematically. The subject matter should be interesting and at the same time the likes and dislikes of the students should also be considered. The topics and subtopics should be organized with proper numbering and appropriate titles.

The illustrations occupy most of the content in science books. In morphology or anatomy or any other sub-topics the illustrations play a major role. The illustration should be accompanied by neat labeled diagrams or with photographs.

The language of the textbook should be based on the experience and ability of the students. The words and terms used by the biologists and language experts should be used. The language of the textbook should be based on the language of the students. The subject matter should be written in a simple and clear language. As for as possible the biological terms should be used according to the nature of the mother tongue. If it is possible English terms can be used in mother tongue without changing the pronunciation. For example terms like cell, tissue, protoplasm and mitochondria can be used in Tamil as they are. The English terms can be given within brackets. When mother tongue terms are used, they should be based on the terms used in state and central education departments. The terms, which give two meanings, should not be used in biology textbooks. Lengthy sentences can be avoided and short and brief sentences can be used. The sentences which explain the meaning directly should be used.

NEED AND SIGNIFICANCE OF TEXTBOOK ANALYSIS

Kothari commission states that, "the fact that the science subject which is not taught clearly and which is learnt in a worse situation is more ridiculous than creating mere information about the subject in the mind of young children". Thus, there should be qualitative improvement with regarding the text books so that the standards achieved are adequate, kept continually raising and become internationally comparable. Hence the evaluation of textbooks is necessary to achieve such standards.

For ages books have been deemed to be the most reliable means of storing information. In the teaching-learning process teachers and students have been using several tools. Among these tools textbooks are one of the studying tools which take place in the printed and published tools group and serve as a source for students' learning lives. They are tools which are prepared to make students learn, on their own, the information related to course subjects, in an ordered and correct way. The first books which were produced to be used in schools appeared in 1750s and more commonly in 1770s. Although textbooks have gone through serious changes in terms of design, function etc. Until today, they have not lost their strategic roles in the process of education. One of the most determining and guiding tools in planned and a programmed educational study is again textbooks.

Textbook is the published work used for educational purposes, which will be used in formal and non-formal educational institutions of any kind and at all grades, the chapters of which are prepared in the line with the curricula. It is such a nuclear that it will turn into fruits which will help to improve, in the student, the communication skills such as thinking, interpreting, listening, speaking, reading and writing; positive social attitudes; pleasure of working; respect for human values and the feeling of fraternity between nations. When considered from the view of education technology components it is observed that textbooks are only one of the many tools and method types which take place among non-human sources.

Education is a continuous process for acquiring experience. Newer type of experience is gathered in the world of knowledge. Like the developed countries of the world textbook evaluation is badly needed to mobilize the acquisition of knowledge in developing countries also. To acquire the main goal of curriculum suitable textbook has a greater responsibility. Textbook will be developed according to the age, capability, desire, interest of the learner so that the learner can perceive the subject matter easily.

Students and teachers are highly dependent on textbook. Aims and objectives of the curriculum are directly reflected through a textbook. So the development of textbook is required to achieve the assigned aims and objectives set in the curriculum. If the textbook had been developed according to the curriculum, it would have probable that students would achieve expected aims and objectives. And textbook evaluation is a major part of textbook development.

CONCEPT OF EDUCATION

According to thinkers in India "Vidya" or Knowledge or learning or education is the 'third eye' of the man which gives him an insight into all affairs and teaches him how to act; it leads us to our salvation: in the mundane sphere it leads us to all round progress and prosperity. The uses of education are too diverse to be enumerated exhaustively. It is veritable desire yielding tree.

Joseph Addison (1672- 1719) believed "what Sculpture is to a block of marble, education is to a human soul"

The word education has a very wide connation. It is like a diamond which appears to be different color when seen from a different angle. Like the concept proverbial elephant as described by blind man, an artist, a biologist, an economist, an educator, a philosopher, a political leader psychologist and sociologist etc. Seems to have his own concept meaning of education which is influenced by his own out work of life. Etymologically the word 'education is derived from the Latin word 'Educare' this implies 'to draw out', 'to lead out'. 'Educatum' denotes 'to train' the education means to bring up, to draw out the lead out, to nourish, and to rise, to train.

A Synthesis of the meaning of these terms implies that education is drawing out and leading out. Something from within the raising and training.

Dr. Radha Krishnan defined education on "Training the intellect, refinement of the heart and discipline of the spirit".

Gandhi has defined education as "By education I mean all round drawing out of the best in child and man body, mind and spirit".

In the process of education, three important elements are prominent. Those are the "educated" or the child who is to be "educated" the "educators" or the teacher who provides opportunities and organized learning experience for Childs education and the "social setting" and foreign which the process of education to carried on.

The Aim of Education

The search for aims in education is a perennial one. The historical perspective of Brahmanism, Buddhist and Islamic system of education are a well balanced personality. This should be the result of good education system.

According to secondary education commission (1952- 53) the secret of good education consists in enabling the students to realize what are his talents and aptitudes and in what manner and to what they can best develop them so as to achieve proper social adjustment and seek right types of employment. Education should therefore produce a well balanced personality rather than a lopsided individual.

Regunath Safaya .D Shaida (1994) has quoted in their book on "Development of Educational Theory and Practice" that ultimate aim of all training according to Swami Vivekananda is man making. Every child as it comes to the world is not man, in the real sense of term. It is only through education and training that his individuality is transformed into the personality of man fit for his civilized of the times.

TEXTBOOKS AND SCIENCE LEARNING

Given the impact of textbooks on learning, because textbooks are one of the primary sources from which students obtain knowledge, the inadequate and inconsistent scientific knowledge presented in science textbooks will negatively affect students' ideas (Irez, 2009). He also argues that uniformed ideas presented in a textbook could affect students' learning in a direct or indirect way. The focus of this paper will be the analysis of the selected textbooks in the light of possible misconceptions that can be induced during students' learning process, and the structure and characteristics of text and pictorial elements that are presented in the textbook.

Valverde, Bianchi, Wolfe, Schmidt, and Houang (2002:1) stated that "Textbooks help define school subjects as students experience them. They represent school disciplines to students". Textbooks also facilitate topic selection by teachers and provide an orientation in the way these topics are taught (Martínez-Gracia, Gil-Quílez, & Osada, 2006). Many teachers also rely on the textbook in deciding what and how to teach, especially when they are teaching outside their area of expertise (Stern & Roseman, 2004). Textbook authors have freedom to develop their own approach to the delivery of national curricula and examination specifications, and so textbooks represent a considerable diversity (Martínez-Gracia et al., 2006). Concern has been expressed that information in text books is not always found to be accurate (Clifford, 2002). It is also important to emphasise that teachers, as facilitators of learning, should be aware of the problems and limitations of the text book their students are using (Haggarty & Pepin, 2002).

Science Learning With Textbooks

A cognitive theory of multimedia learning (Mayer, 1997) suggests that in multimedia learning the learner engages in three important cognitive processes. The first cognitive process, selecting, is applied to incoming verbal information to yield a text base and is applied to incoming visual information to yield an image base. The second cognitive process, organizing, is applied to the word base to create a verbally-based model of the to-be-explained system, and is applied to the image base to create a visually-based model of the to-be-explained system. Both processes should be used by the learner when using the textbook. Finally, the third process, integrating, occurs when the learner builds connections between corresponding events (or states or parts) in the verbally-based model and the visually-based model. This theory suggests that it is better to present an explanation in words and pictures together than solely in words. This is also confirmed by different studies (Levie & Lentz, 1982; Vasu & Howe, 1989) that emphasize a combination of both visual and verbal methods as being ideal. Visual-verbal learning allows students to reconcile the two modes and compare carefully the information available in the picture with the explanation in the text (Reid, Briggs, & Beveridge, 1983).

Considerable attention has been devoted to the effect of visual learning on the acquisition of knowledge and the understanding of relationships and processes in science education (Mandl & Levin, 1989). Illustrations are the basis of visual learning in the science classroom and include representations found in typical science textbooks, such as photographs, diagrams, charts, graphs, drawings, and tables (Cook, 2008). In a study of six science textbooks, Mayer (1993) found that 55% of the printed space was accounted for by illustrations. Cook (2008) suggested that because illustrations are a large part of science textbooks, more attention must be focused on understanding the impact visual images have on students and their learning. Ametller and Pinto (2002) summarised that visual presentations play a very important role in the communication of science concepts.

Research also shows (Dimopoulos, Koulaidis, & Sklaveniti, 2003) that images contribute to the higher level of meaning of the text. They also concluded that modern textbooks integrate more images in the text than did textbooks in the past. This indicates the influence of modern technologies that facilitate the application of different visualization materials to present science and technology through media. Visualization material is often a quite transparent and unproblematic method to represent reality and communicate science and technology. On the other hand, Stylianidou, Ormerod and Ogborn (2002) summarised that images could present additional problems for students' understanding the message of the specific topic explained in the textbook, so they emphasise that more attention should be paid to construct the pictorial representations for textbooks, especially by: (1)

mixing the symbolic and real entities in an image (hybrid image), (2) highlighting some elements of the image, (3) encoding different meanings of similar symbols in different ways, (4) constructing and placing of the verbal elements in the image, (5) paying attention to the layout when one image is created by several pictures, and (6) realizing that compositional structures are used to read meaning into images.

However, students also have difficulty in identifying and understanding the concepts that are unique to particular science phenomena. Therefore, pictorial material must include information to elicit students' prior knowledge, and information to foster comprehension of new concepts presented in a textbook. It is also important that the colours used in illustrations be carefully selected, since many students interpret differently the colours representing different features in the picture (Cook, 2008).

Research also shows that around 90% of students learn science using some form of text, but important conclusions are that science texts do not significantly contribute to quality learning in science education (Peacock & Gates, 2000). Science textbooks demand that the learner integrates quite complicated science concepts, together with language abilities (scientific vocabulary and syntax and also capability of reading, writing and oral communicating), visualization materials (different images, symbols, comic-strip style) and format in the science text. They are multi-modal texts made up of different expressive methods (Lemke, 1998). Textbooks also describe links between real world phenomena and scientific theories (Ahtineva, 2005) and determine the content to be taught as well as basic guidelines for teaching procedures. Trends in International Mathematics and Science Study (TIMSS) showed that about 50% of weekly teaching time is used by teachers to teach by textbooks (Wang, 1998).

Curriculum and Textbooks Development

It is also recommended that the learning goals stated in the national curriculum should lead the content analysis of the educational material (Kesidou & Roseman, 2002). Curriculum material research suggests that curriculum development drives the assessment development, and that assessment is designed to align to the actual content included in the learning material. Such a statement could be accepted because a lot of assessment tasks appear tailored to fit incidental details of the learning material rather than some important generalisation of scientific ideas to be remembered by students at the end of a learning process (Stern & Ahlgren, 2002).

Teacher and Textbooks

An important aspect is also the teachers' ability to critically analyse curriculum materials, because the teacher should have the authority and resources to select the most appropriate materials and to take the decision about when, where and how to make them useful for his/her teaching (Wang, 1998).

Research shows that students differently recognize the objects depicted in the illustrations presented in textbooks (Constable, Campbell, & Brown, 1988), and that many illustrations in textbooks depicting science processes assume prior knowledge on the part of the student (Cook, 2008). Cook (2008) stated that teachers often anticipate that most students understand the visual images presented in science textbooks, but Billings and Klanderman (2000) pointed out that student misconceptions can be generated in the process of interpreting illustrations, and many stem from the lack of prior experience with the subject in their daily lives (Wu, Krajcik, & Soloway, 2001). Teachers must help students to develop the basic skills of visual communication, specifically by teaching them to critically evaluate the form and content of visual communication (Cook, 2008). Students need to be taught how to read illustrations in order to avoid potential causes of confusion (Stylianidou et al., 2002), and teachers need to be aware of students' difficulties when reading images (Ametller & Pinto, 2002).

Science textbooks are among commonly used effective teaching materials in science education process that it seems a significant source of conceptual problems have been detected on pupils. So many researchers (Abimbola & Baba, 1996; Barras, 1984; Cho, Kahle & Nordland, 1985; Rees, 2007; Storey, 1989, 1991, 1992) have made a systematic effort to define alternative conceptions or misconceptions in biology textbooks. It is well known that educators have always taken textbooks into consideration as a good source of information. Odom (1993) has been searched how the concepts related with action potentials are presented in high school biology textbooks and alternative conceptions related with this subject. Sewell (2002) identified a major problem with science textbooks that they too often contain many alternative conceptions and false ideas. Dikmenli and

Çardak (2004) have been determined 14 alternative conceptions and 10 inadequate knowledge about cell structure and functions in high school 1st class biology textbooks that may lead to alternative conceptions. Hershey (2004, 2005) has been stated that any alternative conception existing in a textbook, article or curriculum program may mislead many teachers or students and classified over 50 alternative conceptions determined in written materials related with plants in 5 categories. These categories were; oversimplifications, overgeneralizations, obsolete concepts and terms, misidentifications and flawed research. Köse, Ayas, Costu, and Karamustafaoglu (2004) evaluated how the topic of photosynthesis is presented in a high school biology textbook on the basic views of teachers and specialists. In this study researchers have been concluded that photosynthesis topic is incorrectly included in the textbook and some scientific faults were available. Similarly, Schussler (2008) has been searched how the topic of fertilization in plants is presented and for alternative conception about this topic in 61 science books prepared for children. The researcher evidenced that pollination-fertilization and ovule-egg terms are used in a misleading way in these books. In addition, it was also stated that the term "pollen dust" used in the books is not a botanical term and used incorrectly.

Because, insufficiency of teaching technology and laboratory deficiency and applying traditional teaching strategies in developing countries makes textbooks more dominant teaching material. In this countries science and technology textbooks are the central tool in the instructional process of teaching science. For example, Chiappetta, Ganesh, Lee and Philips (2006) noted that more than 90% of secondary school science teachers rely on textbooks to organize and deliver instruction and assign homework. On the other hand, textbook authors have freedom to develop their own approach to the delivery of national curricula and so textbooks represent a considerable diversity. Concern has been expressed that information in textbooks is not always found to be accurate (Clifford, 2002). It is important for teachers, as facilitators of learning, to be aware of the conceptual problems of the textbook their students are using.

Anderson, (1980) studied on **"How clearly written are Children's Textbooks or, of Bladderworts and Alfa"**. Two representative samples of expository prose from sixth grade textbooks (one in science and one in social studies) were analyzed for clarity of explanation. Four text criteria were applied to the analyses: structure, unity, coherence, and audience appropriateness. The results of the analysis suggested that many children's textbooks are not clearly written. It was proposed that the procedures commonly used by authors to make texts easier to read (shorter sentences, easier vocabulary, less detail, and use of condensed explanations of ideas) may instead cause the text to be even more difficult to comprehend. The effect of poor quality text on how well children learn to read and comprehend text may also be very great. A third suggestion, based on these research results, is that poorly written texts may develop undesirable student attitudes toward reading texts. To combat these possible effects of poorly written texts, it was proposed that editors and publishers monitor textbook production more carefully, that teachers evaluate texts carefully and help students develop textbook reading skills, and that authors of textbooks pay closer attention to structure, coherence, unity, and audience appropriateness.

JOSE C. OTERO, (1990) studied on "**Comprehension Evaluation and Regulation in Learning from Science Texts**". Metacognitive variables influence students' learning from science texts. This article deals with the comprehension monitoring abilities of secondary school science students, one of the aims of metacognition which has drawn considerable attention from researchers. The aims of the study are, in particular: (a) to know the extent to which comprehension is monitored by secondary science students as revealed by inconsistency detection in manipulated science texts. And (b) to identify the strategies used to regulate comprehension by the students who detect the inconsistencies. The results indicate that knowing that are understands or fails to understand science texts could be as important a problem as understanding proper. Besides, some incorrect regulatory strategies used by students who notice the inconsistencies in the texts are identified. These could also have an annoying influence in the regulatory behavior of students when studying regular science texts.

Norman G. Lederman, (1992) studied on "**Students' and Teachers' Conceptions of the Nature of Science**". The development of adequate student conceptions of the nature of science has been a perennial objective of science instruction regardless of the currently advocated pedagogical or curricular emphases. Consequently, it has been an area of prolific research characterized by several parallel, but distinct, lines of investigation. Although research related to students' and teachers' conceptions of the nature of science has been conducted for approximately 40 years, a comprehensive review of the empirical literature (both quantitative and qualitative) has yet to be presented. The overall purpose of this review is to help clarify what has been learned and to elucidate the basic assumptions and logic which have guided earlier research efforts. Ultimately, recommendations related to both methodology and the focuses of future research are offered.

Eugene L. Chiappetta,(1993) studied on **"Do Middle School Life Science Textbooks provide a Balance of Scientific Literacy Themes"**. Four themes of scientific literacy have been synthesized to analyze science textbooks for this purpose: (a) science as a body of knowledge, (b) science as a way of investigating, (c) science as a way of thinking, and (d) the interaction among science, technology, and society (STS). The intercoder agreement between two researchers who coded the units of analysis for the four themes was high. The life science textbooks examined in this study seem to stress two aspects of scientific literacy—science as a body of knowledge and science as a way of investigating. These textbooks devote practically no text to science as a way of thinking. Very little text is devoted to the interaction of science, technology, and society. There was at least one chapter in each textbook that addressed the nature of science and its relationship to life science. Most of the analyzed textbooks present the stereotypical steps of the scientific method and do not provide a balance of scientific literacy themes.

Vasilis Koulaidis, (1996) studied on **"A Pedagogical Analysis of Science Textbooks"**. This paper discusses some of the available frameworks for the pedagogical analysis of school science textbooks. First, it distinguishes between (a) studies which focus on elements of textbooks, such as the content, vocabulary, illustrations used, and the teaching methods promoted; and (b) those which consider the principles that organize the content and the form of presentation. In attempting to consider the sorts of principles that may be used in the studies categorised under (b), two crucial issues are discussed. The first issue refers to the relationship between scientific knowledge and school knowledge, which, as the relevant literature suggests, might not be conceived merely as a simplified "casting" of the scientific structure, but rather should be understood as a complex social process. The second issue explicitly addresses the nature of the pedagogic relationship and the place of the pedagogic text within it. Recent views about the nature of knowledge, it is argued, would suggest a reconceptualisation of the teaching activity, and indicate a model according to which the three elements of the teaching situation-the content, the pupil and the teacher-are seen as being (re)constituted in their articulation within and through the textbook. Thus, for example, what is to be a competent pupil in this approach is a function of the text. On the basis of these considerations, three approaches to the analysis of science textbooks are discussed: the socio-cognitive, the sociolinguistic and the socio-epistemic. The relative merits of the third approach are considered, and some examples are used from Greek science textbooks.

Luli Stern, (2004) studied on **"Can Middle-School Science Textbooks Help Students Learn Important Ideas".** The transfer of matter and energy from one organism to another and between organisms and their physical setting is a fundamental concept in life science. Not surprisingly, this concept is common to the *Benchmarks for Science Literacy* (American Association for the Advancement of Science, 1993), the *National Science Education Standards* (National Research Council, 1996), and most state frameworks and likely to appear in any middle-school science curriculum material. Nonetheless, while topics such as photosynthesis and cellular respiration have been taught for many years, research on student learning indicates that students have difficulties in learning these ideas. In this study, nine middle-school curriculum materials—both widely used and newly developed—were examined in detail for their support of student learning ideas concerning matter and energy transformations in ecosystems specified in the national standards documents.

The analysis procedure used in this study was previously developed and field tested by Project 2061 of the AAAS on a variety of curriculum materials. According to our findings, currently available curriculum materials provide little support for the attainment of the key ideas chosen for this study.

In general, these materials do not take into account students' prior knowledge, lack representations to clarify abstract ideas, and are deficient in phenomena that can be explained by the key ideas and hence can make them plausible. This article concludes with a discussion of the implications of this study to curriculum development, teaching, and science education research based on shortcomings in today's curricula.

Mushtaq Ahmed I. Patel, (2007) studied on "**An Evaluation of Environmental Science II Textbooks of Third and Fourth Standards of Andhra Pradesh**". The investigators have attempted to evaluate Environmental Science II (EVS II) textbook with the help of specially constructed rating scale. In this rating scale the areas covered included organization of matter, contents of the textbooks, accuracy of text material, indications of teaching aids, illustrations used, psychological soundness, and learning activities. The investigators contacted 50 teachers of Andhra Pradesh who were teaching EVA II of third and fourth standard. The data obtained from the respondents were subjected to percentage analysis. The results shows that the textbooks have properly organized content, which is presented well; the subject matter has accurate information and the situations and illustrations used belong to rural and urban background. The textbook has helped the teachers in deciding about the teaching aids, the illustrations given are appropriate, the matter presented is psychological sound and appropriate learning activities are presented.

Abd-El-Khalick, (2008) studied on "**Representations of Nature of Science in High School Chemistry Textbooks over the Past Four Decades**". This study assessed the representations of nature of Science (NOS) in high school chemistry textbooks and the extent to which these representations have changed during the past four decades. Analyses focused on the empirical, tentative, inferential, creative, theory-driven, and social NOS, in addition to the myth of "The Scientific Method," the nature of scientific theories and laws, and the social and cultural embeddedness of science. A total of 14 textbooks, including five "series" spanning one to four decades, were analyzed. The textbooks commanded significant market shares in the United States and were widely used in some of the most popular states. Relevant textbook sections were scored on each of the target NOS aspects on a scale ranging from -3 to +3, which reflected the accuracy, completeness, and manner (explicit versus implicit) in which these aspects were addressed. The textbooks fared poorly in their representations of NOS. Additionally, with a few exceptions, textbook scores either did not change or decreased over the past four decades. These trends are incommensurate with the discourse in national and international science education reform documents, which has witnessed an increasing emphasis on the centrality of NOS to scientific literacy and pre-college science education during the same time period. Assessment and evaluation strategies and policies need to be targeted if substantial and desired changes in the ways NOS is addressed in science textbooks are to be effected.

Miriam Lemmer, (2008) studied on **"Educators' Selection and Evaluation of Natural Science Textbooks"**. Due to central role of textbooks in the teaching of science, it is imperative that textbooks provide correct content and instructional support. We investigated how 16 South Africa Grade 7 natural science educators selected their textbooks and how they evaluated these textbooks. The results were analyzed according to the constructivist paradigm, as implemented in the Revised National Curriculum Statement, as well as selection criteria found in the literature. The selection criteria that the educators listed in interviews were isolated ideas that were not embedded in a constructivist framework. The educators also lacked that were not embedded in a constructivist framework. The educators also lacked the necessary scientific and pedagogical content-knowledge to effectively evaluate the textbooks. Recommendations are made for improvements in educator training, developmental guidance, and textbook writing. Experience in textbook evaluation during their training course could boost educators' competence in selecting the books and detecting and compensating for their deficiencies. This would contribute to filling South Africa educators' need of hands-on examples that can be applied immediately in their classrooms.

Musa Dikmenli, (2009) studied on **"Conceptual Problems in Biology-Related Topics in Primary Science and Technology Textbooks in Turkey"**. Determination of conceptual problems which may cause alternative conceptions in science and technology textbooks is significant to increase in success of pupils and teachers. It is a vital issue to arrange books in a way removing or decreasing these faults in order to improve a better education via textbooks. This study aims to determine conceptual problems which may cause alternative conceptions in biology topics in science and technology textbooks of primary schools. In this study, the units of each textbook were analyzed page by page according to document examination method and conceptual problems were determined. The founded conceptual problems have been classified such as; misidentifications, overgeneralizations, oversimplifications, obsolete concepts and terms, under generalizations. The finding of research results have been shown that various conceptual problems which may cause alternative conceptions in pupils' textbooks about biology topics. The obtained results of research were compared with related literature and in the light of findings some recommendations were developed for future planning and development activities pupils' textbooks.

Iztok Devetak,(2009) studied on "**States of Matter Explanations in Slovenian Textbooks for Students Aged 6 to 14**". The basic aim of this study is to investigate the content of textual and pictorial material of Slovenian science textbooks and notebooks on topic states of matter. The paper presents the results of the analysis of educational material from two randomly selected publishers for students aged 6 to 14 in the Slovenian primary and the lower secondary school. One topic area (states of matter) was selected to be analysed. The first part of the analysis includes exercise and images analysis according to the selected framework, and the second one content analysis identifying key concepts and connections between them according to the national curriculum recommendations. Results show quite a few similarities between the analysed programmes (number of pages, type of items) but some differences could be detected when comparing the type of images in the educational material. The content analysis of the selected textbooks also shows that they retain the content directed by the national curriculum, but the ways (examples, content of the images etc.) in which authors present the topic differ.

Khalid Mahmood, (2009) studied on "**Textbook Evaluation Through Quality Indicators: The Case of Pakistan**". Curriculum is the main course of action that can ensure the supply of effective and efficient human resource for the development of a nation and a progressive society. Textbooks are the visible, tangible and practical manifestation of the curriculum. These are designed to teach students what the educators believe must be taught. Textbook development and evaluation has always been the subject of debate in Pakistan, due to a variety of reasons. One of the major reasons in this regard is non-availability of explicit criteria for textbook evaluation. The study was designed to identifying indicators of quality textbooks and developing criteria for review, evaluation and approval of quality textbooks in Pakistan. Considering textbook as a product, Garvin's (1988) framework for quality products was used as basis for identification of the indicators and Delphi technique was employed to reach to consensus on them. Based on final indicators, a textbook evaluation criterion was developed. To make the criterion explicit, rubrics for each compliance indicator was developed.

Delgato, Margaret H. (2009) studied on **"Considerations of Multicultural Science And Curriculum Reform: A Content Analysis of State-Adopted Biology Textbooks in Florida"**. The purpose of this investigation was to determine the extent to which multicultural science education, including indigenous knowledge representations, had been infused within the content of high school biology textbooks. The study evaluated the textbook as an instructional tool and framework for multicultural science education instruction by comparing the mainstream content to indigenous knowledge perspectives portrayed in the student and teacher editions of 34 textbooks adopted in Florida within the last four adoption cycles occurring from 1990 to 2006. The investigation involved a content analysis framed from a mixed methods approach. Emphasis was placed, in consideration of the research questions and practicality of interpreting text with the potential for multiple meanings, within qualitative methods. The investigation incorporated five strategies to assess the extent of multicultural content: (1) calculation of frequency of indigenous representations through the use of a tally; (2) assessment of content in the teacher editions by coding the degree of incorporation of multicultural content; (3) development of an archaeology of statements to determine the ways in which indigenous representations were incorporated into the content; (4) use of the Evaluation Coefficient Analysis (ECO) to determine extent of multicultural terminologies within content; and (5) analysis of visuals and illustrations to gauge percentages of depictions of minority groups. Results indicated no solid trend in an increase of inclusion of multicultural content over the last four adoption cycles. Efforts at most reduced the inclusion of indigenous representations and other multicultural content to the level of the teacher edition distributed among the teacher-interleafed pages or as annotations in the margins. Degree of support of multicultural content to the specific goals and objectives remained limited across all four of the adoption cycles represented in the study. Emphasis on standardized testing appeared in the six textbooks representing the most recent adoption cycle. Recommendations included increased efforts to identify quality of content by including input from scholars in the field of multicultural education as well as indigenous peoples in the creation of textbook content. Recommendations also included further clarification of the definition of "science" within multicultural science education frameworks, "indigenous knowledge" as compared to "Western science" and "pseudoscience", and "scientific literacy" as a central focus to a multicultural science education meant to address the needs of an increasingly diverse student population and prime-age workforce.

Erdogan, (2009) studied on **"Components of Environmental Literacy in Elementary Science Education Curriculum in Bulgaria and Turkey"**. The purpose of this study was to analyze the extent to which science education objectives in elementary schools addressed to the six basic components of environmental literacy (EL), and how this attention differed from Bulgaria to Turkey. The main method in the study involved comparative content analysis of these objectives. The courses sampled for Bulgaria include "The Human Being and Nature", "Biology and Health Education", "Chemistry and Environmental Protection" and "Physics and Astronomy". The course sampled for Turkey is "Science and Technology Education". Content analysis of these objectives reveals that all components of environmental literacy did not receive the same attention. For example in both countries most attention was given to knowledge, less to skills and attitudes, and little to environmentally responsible behavior (ERB).

Gonzalez-Rodriguez, (2009) studied on **"Plant Nutrition in Spanish Secondary Textbooks"**. In this paper, the authors analyse the conceptual contents related to plant nutrition in the widely-used school texts of six Spanish publishers. An analysis dossier was elaborated based on the epistemological and pedagogical study of this subject. The publishers deal with the issue of plant nutrition at three different levels (multicellular, cellular and ecosystem) and they establish a conceptual progression. Furthermore, they include a great number of concepts which they deal with in the texts. However, not all of the texts promote the development of a global conception of plant nutrition.

Kahveci, (2010) studied on **"Quantitative Analysis of Science and Chemistry Textbooks for Indicators of Reform: A Complementary Perspective"**. In this study, multiple thematically based and quantitative analysis procedures were utilized to explore the effectiveness of Turkish chemistry and science textbooks in terms of their reflection of reform. The themes gender equity, questioning level, science vocabulary load, and readability level provided the conceptual framework for the analyses. An unobtrusive research method, content analysis, was used by coding the manifest content and counting the frequency of words, photographs, drawings, and questions by cognitive level. The context was an undergraduate chemistry teacher preparation program at a large public university in a metropolitan area in northwestern Turkey. Forty preservice chemistry teachers were guided to analyze 10 middle school science and 10 high school chemistry textbooks. Overall, the textbooks included unfair gender representations, a considerably higher number of input and processing than output level questions, and high load of science terminology. The textbooks failed to provide sufficient empirical evidence to be considered as gender equitable and inquiry-based. The quantitative approach employed for evaluation contrasts with a more interpretive approach, and has the potential in depicting textbook profiles in a more reliable way, complementing the commonly employed qualitative procedures. Implications suggest that further work in this line is needed on calibrating the analysis procedures with science textbooks used in different international settings. The procedures could be modified and improved to meet specific evaluation needs. In the Turkish context, next step research may concern the analysis of science textbooks being rewritten for the reform-based curricula to make cross-comparisons and evaluate a possible progression.

Slough, Scott W. (2010) studied on **"Science Textbooks' Use Of Graphical Representation: A Descriptive Analysis Of Four Sixth Grade Science Texts"**. Middle school teachers tend to rely heavily on texts that have become increasing more visual. There is little information available about the graphical demands of general middle grades' science texts. The purpose of this study was to quantify the type and quality of the graphical representations and how they interacted with the textual material in middle school science texts. Four State of Texas-approved sixth-grade science texts were examined using a researcher-developed instrument, Graphical Analysis Protocol (GAP). Results produced reasons for concern (least analytic forms of graphics dominated, one third of all graphics were decorative in nature, most graphics were static in nature, and approximately one third were not connected to the text spatially or semantically) and reasons for optimism (approximately one third of the time more analytic forms of graphics were used, two thirds served a specific cognitive function, and over half of the graphics were connected to the text and indexically referenced). Further research is warranted on a larger sample of texts from different states, publishers, grade levels, and subjects. It is also important to establish a connection to increased student learning and/or teacher preference due to higher incidences of any of the variables or principles that make up the GAP instrument.

Rillero, Peter (2010) studied on **"The Rise and Fall of Science Education: A Content Analysis of Science in Elementary Reading Textbooks of the 19th Century"**. In the 19th century the textbook dominated the curriculum and methods of instruction. The most important textbook was the textbook of reading known as the reader. In the early 1800s science was not established as a separate primary grade subject. The science students encountered in these reading textbooks may have been their only formal science education. This study used content analysis to determine the type of science and the quantity of science in popular U.S. readers of the 19th century. The percent of science rose in the middle of the century and declined at the end. This decline may have been due to the desire to make the study of reading literary based. The percentage of science that was biological increased throughout the century, and the percentage of Earth science declined.

Schussler, (2010) studied on **"Exploring Plant and Animal Content in Elementary Science Textbooks"**. Student knowledge about plants is typically less than student knowledge about animals. Textbooks are a commonly-used curriculum material in elementary grades and contain embedded cultural ideologies that may impact instruction. This study analyzed two nationally-syndicated elementary science textbook series to explore their presentation of plant and animal content. The results indicated that the amount of animal content was greater than plant content in each series. An even greater difference was found in the number of plant and animal examples used within the textbooks. There were more than twice as many animal examples as plant examples in both textbook series, and the most repeated animal examples were more likely to correspond to scientifically-appropriate classification categories. The study also identified differences in the plant and animal topics covered in the textbooks; the topic of plant parts was the plant topic with the highest coverage in each textbook series, while for animals, the topics of animal needs, adaptations and types had the highest coverage depending on the textbook series. This study suggests there may be an ideology favoring animals within these elementary science textbooks and that teachers need to supplement their instruction with additional plant information to facilitate student learning about plants.

Gericke, (2010) studied on "**Conceptual Variation in the Depiction of Gene Function in Upper Secondary School Textbooks**". This paper explores conceptual variation in the depiction of gene function in upper secondary school textbooks. Historically, concepts in genetics have developed in various scientific frameworks, which has led to a level of incommensurability as concepts have changed over time within their respective frameworks. Since students may have difficulties in understanding concepts where there is implicit variation in descriptions of the same phenomena, we have developed a concept mapping instrument and applied it to study the gene function concepts in biology and chemistry textbooks that are widely used in Sweden, and others used in a selection of English speaking countries. The data were then further examined using content analysis. In the present paper we describe the conceptual variation of gene function as it is presented in the textbooks, and analyze the ways in which students' understanding may be influenced. We conclude that it may be difficult for students to gain a modern, process-oriented understanding of gene function if textbooks are used as foundations for the planning and execution of lessons.

Arup Ratan Das, (2011) studied on "**An Evaluation of the Environmental Studies: Science Textbooks and Teachers' Guides Used in BRAC Primary Schools**". The objective of this study was to do an evaluation of science textbooks and teachers' guides of grade I-V used in BRAC Primary Schools. Only qualitative approach was used here. The study was done through document analysis. Five science textbooks were evaluated here on the basis of a set of selected criteria. This set of criteria was selected through analyzing related literature and consultation with experts. Here, BRAC was using their own developed textbooks for grade I, II & III and textbooks of National Curriculum and Textbook Board (NCTB) for grade IV & V. Study findings showed that criteria of a standardized textbook were found to be mostly evident in BRAC own textbooks. On the contrary, they were found to be moderately evident in NCTB textbooks. Thus, by comparing strength and weakness of these books, the study had recommended some tasks for revising current textbooks, and developing standardized science textbooks.

Michelle Cook, (2011) studied on "**Teachers' use of Visual Representations in the Science Classroom**". In the current science education literature, most of the attention has focused on understanding the impact visual representations in textbooks and multimedia materials have on students and their learning, but very few studies have focused on teachers' use of these graphics in the classroom. The purpose of this study is to investigate how seven high school science teachers use visual representations in their teaching. A case study approach was used in this research. First, mini-cases were developed to examine the research question from the participants' perspective; then, a cross-case analysis was used to examine the similarities and differences among participants to develop an overarching case in order to understand the factors involved with teachers' use of visual representations. The findings of this study indicate that course content, student characteristics, and resource availability affect how teachers select and use graphics in their science courses.

Nakiboglu, (2011) studied on "**Analysis of Turkish High School Chemistry Textbooks and Teacher-Generated Questions about Gas Laws**". This study presents the results of an analysis of high school chemistry textbooks and teacher-generated questions about gas laws. The materials that were analyzed consisted of 456 questions about gas laws found in seven grade 10 chemistry textbooks and 264 teacher-generated examination questions prepared by seven chemistry teachers from three schools. These questions were classified into three categories (recall, algorithmic, and conceptual); the conceptual questions (ConQ) were further classified into six subcategories (particulate, demonstration, tiered, laboratory, analogy, and series completion) using the descriptions provided on the Conceptual Questions and Challenge Problems website. The findings indicate that most of the textbook questions were algorithmic and that these textbooks were less likely to facilitate or encourage student comprehension of the properties and behaviors of gases or gas law theories. Furthermore, most of the textbook questions do not enable students to develop conceptual understanding and gain higher-order cognitive skills. Although the findings imply that most of the teacher-generated questions were ConQ, the large majority were partially conceptual type questions. The major implication of this research is the need for teachers, textbook writers, and academics to consider question types when creating questions or analyzing chemistry questions at all educational levels.

Bazzul, (2011) studied on **"The Secret Identity of a Biology Textbook: Straight and Naturally Sexed"**. While education communities have well defined commitments to protect their learners from oppressive instructional materials, discourses of science education are often left unexamined. This analysis/critique employs queer theory as a perspective to look at how one widely used textbook in Ontario schools conceptualizes notions of gender and sexuality. Results indicate the use of discourses that promote exclusively heteronormative constructions of sexuality along with sex/gender binaries. Challenging such oppressive misconceptions of sex/gender and sexuality is discussed.

Gkitzia, (2011) studied on **"Development and Application of Suitable Criteria for the Evaluation of Chemical Representations in School Textbooks"**. The study of Chemistry deals essentially with three types of chemical representations: macro, submicro, and symbolic. Research has consistently shown that students experience difficulties in understanding and interpreting the representations, in making translations between different types of representations, and in constructing them. In this study, we conducted a detailed review of existing presuppositions that define what Chemical Representations are to be included in school textbooks for the purpose of enhancing the student's understanding of Chemistry. We then conducted a detailed analysis of the Chemical Representations included in five Chemistry textbooks. The detailed analysis revealed five criteria for the evaluation of chemical representation used in school textbooks. These criteria (C1-C5) are: (C1) the type of the representation; (C2) the interpretation of the surface features; (C3) their relationship to the text; (C4) the existence and the properties of a caption; (C5) the degree of correlation between the components comprising a multiple representation. The utility of the proposed criteria was then checked against a 10th-grade Greek chemistry textbook. The five criteria cover the basic elements required for a better utilization of chemical representations in the understanding of Chemistry. The five criteria can also be used for the analysis of existing school textbooks and as an authoring tool in designing new Chemistry textbooks.

CRITERIA FOR TEXTBOOK EVALUATION

Content Related Criteria

a) Appropriateness of organization of content
b) Appropriateness of sequencing units
c) Presentation of content in attractive and interesting way
d) Presentation of content according to the maxims and theories of learning
e) Conformity to the prescribed syllabus
f) Adequate subject matters to build up scientific concept
g) Relevance to the need of society and nation
h) Relevance to the need, ability, maturity, readiness and psychology of learner
i) Reflection of the domains of behavior (Cognitive, Affective & Psychomotor)
j) Accuracy and up-to-date-ness of concept
k) Relation with life experience and previous knowledge of learners
l) Free of sex stereotypes
m) Avoidance of prejudicial and controversial facts

Science Related Criteria

a) Use of investigatory approach
b) Development of scientific and logical approach
c) Development of understanding of scientific concept
d) Motivating thinking
e) Scope of developing experimental and problem solving skill

Illustration Related Criteria

a) Adequacy and effectiveness of illustration
b) Use of colorful (real) picture and illustration
c) Providing necessary and relevant illustration and examples
d) Use of illustration and example from learners' environment
f) Appropriate placement of illustration
g) Clearness and legibility of illustration
h) The figures are tied into the textual material by direct reference
i) Labeling of the figures

Participation and Activity Related Criteria

a) Provision for theoretical and practical test

b) Providing sufficient exercises for pupils activity

c) Motivating learning by doing

d) Scope of development of creativity of learner

e) These activities can be performed by utilizing locally available resources

g) The number of activities provided in the textbooks are sufficient

Language Related Criteria

a) Comprehensibility and simpleness of language

b) Readability of text

c) Uniformity of spelling and terminology

d) Correctness of spelling

e) Use of comprehensible vocabulary

Physical Aspect Related Criteria

a) Appropriateness of the format (size, bulk, layout of title page)

b) Appropriateness of the typography (font size, face)

c) Appropriateness of binding

d) Appropriateness of title cover

e) Suitability of stitching

f) Appropriateness of printing legibility

g) Absence of printing mistake

h) Appropriateness of paper

i) Sustainability and safety

Teaching Aids Related Criteria

a) Summaries, questions and problems at the end of the chapters are adequate

b) Reference for teachers and students are annotated

Bernard Berelson defined Content Analysis as "a research technique for the objective, systematic, and quantitative description of manifest content of communications" (Berelson, 74). Content analysis is a research tool focused on the actual content and internal features of media. It is used to determine the presence of certain words, concepts, themes, phrases, characters or sentences within texts or sets of texts and to quantify this presence in an objective manner. Texts can be defined broadly as books, book chapters, essays, interviews, discussions, newspaper headlines and articles, historical documents, speeches, conversations, advertising, theater, informal conversation, or really any occurrence of communicative language. To conduct a content analysis of a text, the text is coded or broken down, into manageable categories on a variety of levels--word, word sense, phrase, sentence, or theme--and then examined using one of content analysis' basic methods: conceptual analysis or relational analysis. The results are then used to make inferences about the messages within the text(s), the writer(s), the audience, and even the culture and time of which these are a part. For example, Content Analysis can indicate pertinent features such as comprehensiveness of coverage or the intentions, biases, prejudices, and oversights of authors, publishers, as well as all other persons responsible for the content of materials

Textbook

In the 10th standard textbook there are eight units dealt with Biology was taken for the analysis viz., Heredity and Evolution, Immune system, Structure and Function of Human Body-Organ systems, Reproduction in Plants, A Representative Study of Mammals, Life Processes, Conservation of Environment, and Waste Water Management.

Content of The Unit 1

The first unit Heredity and Evolution contains the following chapter's viz., Heredity, Variation, Evolution, Speciation, Human Evolution, Evolution Tree, Genetic Engineering, Biotechnology and Cloning, Stem Cell (organ) Culture, Microbial Production, Bio-sensor and Bio-chips, and Science today- Gene therapy.

Evidence of Criteria

From the above list of content it seemed that the contents were sufficient and appropriate for this age level of learners. The contents were sequenced in a logical order. The contents were presented according to the maxims theory of learning such as the know to unknown, easy to hard etc., In addition relation with life experience and previous knowledge of learners was kept on presenting the concept. Presented contents were relevant to the need, ability, maturity, readiness and psychology of learners.

In the topic of evolution there was no detailed account given about the theories of evolution (p-6). Content given in the basic techniques in Genetic engineering is not appropriate. It contains only details about the restriction enzyme and ligase. But other important tools such as foreign DNA, Cloning vectors are not mentioned (p-8).

Learning by doing was emphasized in this chapter. The exercises given in this chapter were helping to improve the inductive approach and observation skill. And also this chapter is rich in verbal and writing exercises. These exercises included filling in the blanks, choose the correct one, freehand writing, etc., Exercise within the text was also present here.

Illustration seemed to be helpful for the learners to understand the concepts easily and clearly. The illustrations given in this chapter are relatively modern. For example, the advanced method of curing the damaged cells is described in Gene Therapy (p-12).

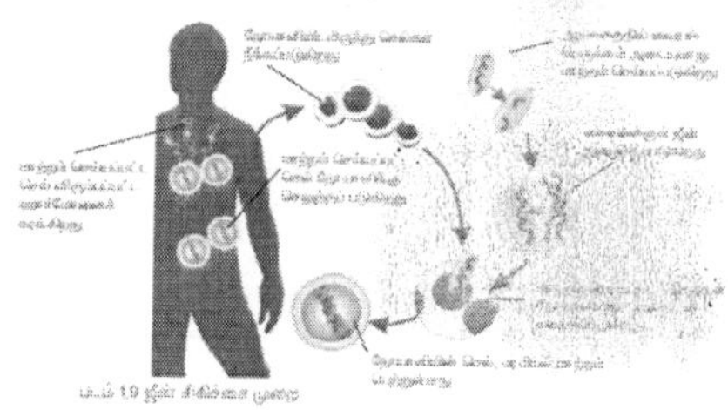

From the illustration 1.1 Seven pairs of contrasting traits in Pea Plant studied by Mendel they failed to differentiate the pod shape and pod color in both the pictures (p-3).

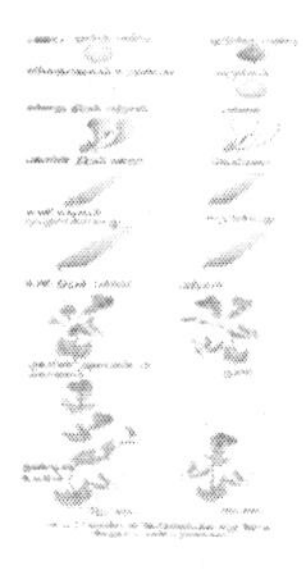

In the topic evolution tree the explanation is provided but could not find out any time description of the evolutionary tree illustration. This will affect the better understanding of the students (p-7).

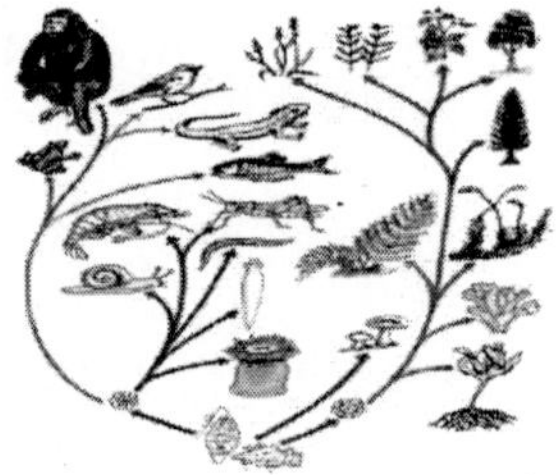

In the illustration Development of Dolly there was no proper labeling for technique of cloning is not mentioned (p-10).

Sentence length, vocabulary and complexity of sentence structure, the factors, which determines the readability of the text, were appropriate in this chapter. Comprehensible vocabulary easy and short length sentences were used in this chapter. In some cases, uniformity is not found in spelling.

பரிணாமம் (P-2)
பரினாமம் (P-32)

ஹோமோ ஹெபிலிஸ் (P-7)
ஹோமியோ ஹேபிலஸ் (P-14)

ஹோமோ எரக்ட்டஸ் (P-7)
ஹோமியோ எரக்ட்டஸ் (P-14)

அல்லீல் (P-4)
அல்லில் (P-13)

அல்லீலோ மார்புகள் (P-4)
அல்லிலோ மார்புகள் (P-13)

ஸ்ட்டிராய்டு (P-9)
ஸ்டிராய்டு (P-14)

பேக்ட்டிரியா (P-11)
பாக்ட்டீரியா (P-19)
பாக்டீரிய்ா (P-32)

டாக்டர்.ஐயான் வில்முட் (P-10)
டாக்டர்.ஐயான் வில்மூட் (P-10)

Content of the Unit 2

The second unit Immune System contains the following chapters viz., Health and its Significance, Diseases and Causes, Diseases caused by microbes and prevention, Modes of transmission, Immunization, Treatment and Prevention, and Biotechnology in medicine.

Evidence of Criteria

From the above list of content it seemed that the contents are sufficient and appropriate for this age level of learners. They were sequenced in a logical order. They are all real life oriented also. The title of the chapter Immune system is not appropriate according to the content. Because this chapter having the conception about diseases and their control only. But the immune system includes organs of the immune system and also the content presented in the text such as types of immunity, disease and their control. So the name of the chapter would be disease and their control instead of immune system. In HIV and Prevention (p-31) no conception about the transmission of the disease is found though it is needed to know to protect learner's themselves.

Learning by doing was emphasized in this chapter. This chapter is rich in verbal and writing exercises. These exercises included filling in the blanks, matching, and freehand writing etc., Exercises within the text also presented here.

Illustrations seemed to be appropriate and helpful for the learners to understand the concepts easily and clearly. Necessary and adequate illustrations are found here. The illustrations used in this chapter are relatively modern. For example Nutritional deficiency diseases are presented through easy and clear illustration (p-18). Some illustrations are not so necessary and unrelated to the text. For example types of viruses are given (p-20) but there is no description found in the text.

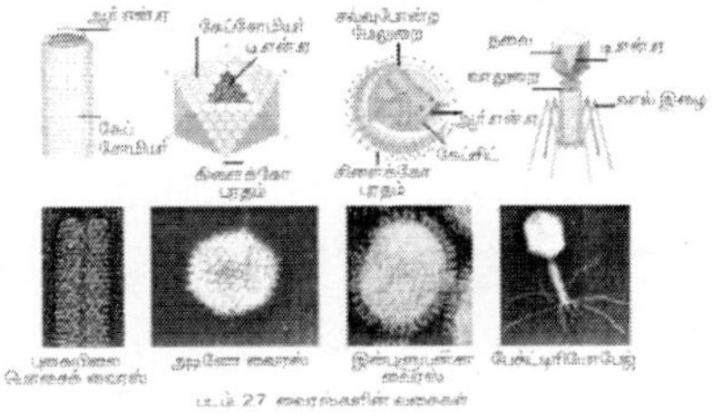

Life cycle of malaria (p-24) is shown through complicated manner. It is very difficult to understand by the learner of this grade.

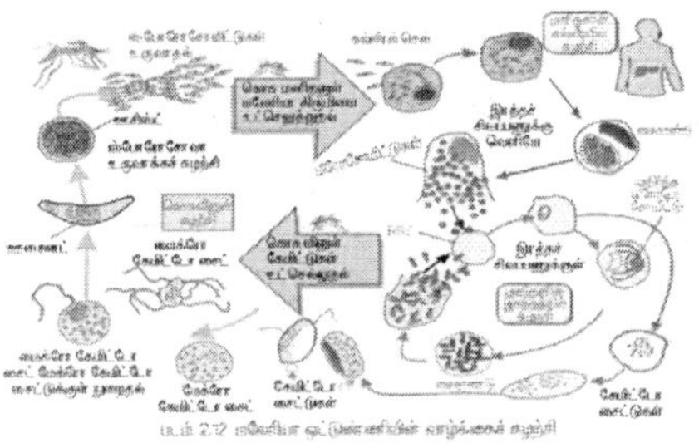

Readability of text seemed to be appropriate in this unit. Comprehensible vocabulary, easy and short length sentences are used in this chapter. In some cases, uniformity in spelling is lacking.

பரிமாணம் (P-16)
பரிமானம் (P-32)

ஹீமோபிலியா (P-18)
ஹீமோபீலீயா (P-33)

டியூபர்குளோசஸ் (P-22)
டியூபர்குளோசிஸ் (P-22)

டைபாய்டு (P-23)
டைப்பாய்டு (P-23, 29)
டைஃபாய்டு (P-142)

அனாபலிஸ் (P-24)
அனாபிலிஸ் (P-24)

பிளாஸ்மோடியம் பால்ஸிபாரம் (P-23)
பிளாஸ்மோடியம் பால்சிபாரம் (P-23, 32)

என்டமிபா ஹிஸ்டலைடிகா (P-25)
என்டமிபா ஹிஸ்டலைட்டிகா (P-32)

டிப்தீரியா (P-26)
டிப்த்தீரியா (P-29)

மீசல்ஸ் (P-26, 29)
மீஸல்ஸ் (P-29)

டெட்டானஸ் (P-29)
டெட்டனஸ் (P-29)

Content of the Unit 3

The third unit Structure and Function of the Human Body-Organ System contains the following chapters viz., Nervous system, Endocrine System, Cell division, and Heredity.

Evidence of Criteria

From the above list of content it seemed that contents are sufficient and appropriate for this age level of learners. They are sequenced in a logical order. Here the title of the unit is Structure and Function of the Human Body-Organ System. But only the conception about Nervous system and Endocrine system is given. Even though in the previous grades the Human Body Organ System unit contains only the conception about Skin, Musculoskeletal system, Digestive system, Circulatory system, Respiratory system and Excretory system alone. The textbook fails to describe about the Sensory organ system.

The pituitary gland is the master gland. So it controls the secretory activities of several other endocrine glands. But in the text it is given as some of the endocrine glands are regulated by the pituitary gland (p-43).

Some inappropriate contents are given in this unit like Cell division and Heredity (p-48). These concepts have to include in the first unit Heredity and Evolution.

Apart from this the information provided for the contents like Nervous system and Endocrine system are very appropriate and sufficient.

Learning by doing was emphasized in this unit. A lot of opportunity for practical work and exercise are found here. For example, in the topic Nervous system and Endocrine system learners will make the model of functioning of the brain, the structure of the neuron and organs of the endocrine system by using clay, cardboard, thermocol, etc., Here the learners can show their creativity through making models and drawing pictures. This unit is rich in verbal, writing and drawing exercises. These exercises included choosing the best answer, fill in the blanks, matching and select the true statement etc.,

Illustrations seemed to be appropriate and helpful for the learners understand the concepts easily and clearly. Necessary and adequate illustrations are found here. The illustrations used in this unit are relatively modern. The photographic reproductions are large and clear. For example, in this unit Nervous system and Organs of Endocrine glands were presented through easy and clear illustration.

Readability of the text seemed to be appropriate in this unit. Comprehensible vocabulary, easy and short length sentences are used in this unit. In some cases, uniformity in spelling is lacking.

டென்டிரைட் (p-37)
டென்ட்ரைட் (p-36)

ஆக்சான் (p-36)
ஆக்ஸான் (p-37)

நிசல் துகள் (p-36)
நிஸில் துகள் (p-37)

ரேன்வியர் கணு (p-36)
ரன்வீர் கணு (p-37)

கார்பஸ் கலோஸம் (p-39)
கார்பஸ் கலோசம் (p-40)

வென்ட்ரிக்கிள் (p-41)

வென்டிக்கிள் (p-41)

பைனியல் (p-42)
பினியல் (p-43)

கணையம் (p-10)
கணயம் (p-43)

டயாபடீஸ் மெல்லிடஸ் (p-46)
டயபட்டிஸ் மெலிடஸ் (p-17)

டையாபெடீஸ் இன்சிபிடஸ் (p-44)
டயபடிஸ் இன்சிபிடிஸ் (p-17)

எபிதீலிய (p-52)
எபிதிலிய (p-48)

சைகோடீன் (p-48)
சைகோட்டின் (p-49, 52)

டிப்ளோடீன் (p-49)
டிப்ளோட்டீன் (p-52)

டயகைனெசிஸ் (p-52)
டையாகைனஸின் (p-49)
டையாகைனகிஸ் (p-48)

மியாஸிஸ் (p-48)
மியாசிஸ் (p-49)
மியசிஸ் (p-49)
மயோசிஸ் (p-50)

சைட்டோகைனசிஸ் (p-50)
சைட்டோகைனஸிஸ் (p-50)

புரோஜெஸ்டீரோன் (p-44)
புரோஜெஸ்டிரான் (p-47)

அட்ரீனல் சுரப்பி (p-46)
அட்ரினல் சுரப்பி (p-47)

Content of the Unit 4

The fourth unit Reproduction in Plants contains the following chapter's viz., Modes of reproduction-vegetative, asexual and sexual reproduction in plants, Pollination, Fertilization, Fruits and seed formation and seed dispersal.

Evidence of Criteria

From the above list of content it seemed that the contents are sufficient and appropriate for this age level of learners. They are all sequenced in a logical order. For example, this unit starts from the mode of reproduction, pollination, fertilization, fruit and seeds the complete life cycle of the plant are given in the sequential order.

Learning by doing was emphasized in this unit. A lot of opportunity for practical work and exercises were found here. For example, by doing the experiment like dissect and display gynoecium, classify fruit berry, and identify the structure of ovule from this experiments the learners gain the both practical and theoretical knowledge about the content. This kind of work could help learners to show their creativity and develop their experimental skill. This unit was rich in verbal and writing exercises. These exercises included filling in the blanks, matching, freehand writing, true/false, choosing right answer, drawing pictures etc., Exercise within the text was also present here.

Illustrations are seemed to be appropriate and helpful for the learners to understand the concepts easily and clearly. Necessary and appropriate illustrations are found here. For example, parts of the flower, classification of fruits etc., Were presented through clear and appropriate size figures. In some cases the labeling of the diagram was inappropriate. For example, an illustration of the complete process of pollination and fertilization (fig4. 2, p-55) was given but there was no proper labeling found here and also the clarity of the picture was very low.

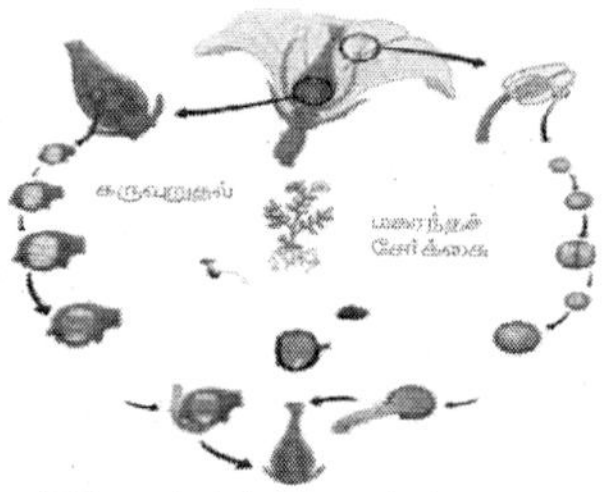

படம்.4.2. மகரந்தச் சேர்க்கை மற்றும் கருவுறுதல்

Diagram of pistil, showing pollination and fertilization is given (fig4.15, p-62) but the major parts such as male gametes, embryo sac and secondary nucleus are not labeled here.

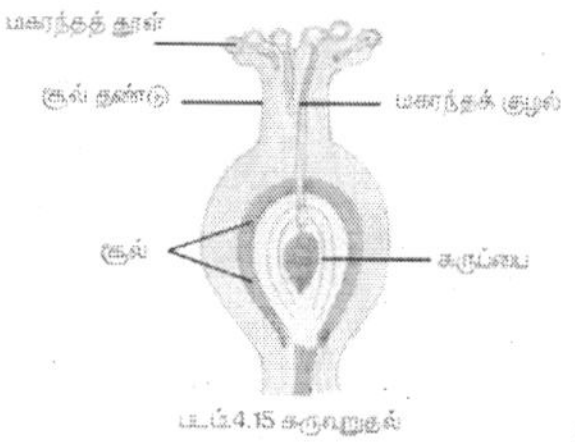

படம்4.15 கருவுறுதல்

Same way illustration for binary fission in amoeba (fig 4.3, p-56) was not labeled properly and also the size of the figure was inappropriate.

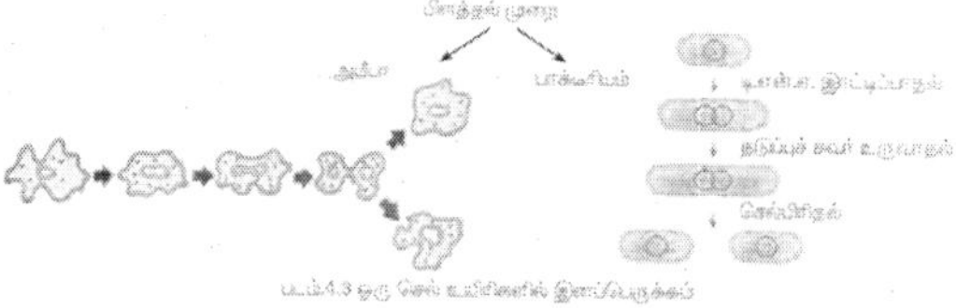

படம்4.3 ஒரு செல் உயிரிகளில் இனப்பெருக்கம்

Some illustrations were not so necessary and unrelated to the text (the life cycle of frog fig 4.1, p-54).

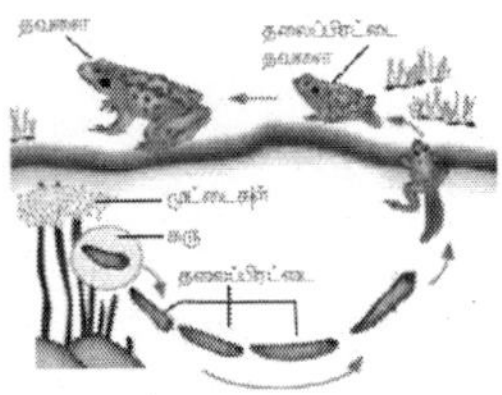

Readability of the text seemed to be appropriate in this unit. Comprehensible vocabulary, easy and short length sentences were used in this unit. In some cases, uniformity in spelling is lacking.

லேக்டோபாசில்லை (p-55)
லேக்டோபேசில்லை (p-55)

எபிளானோஸ்போர்க்கள் (p-57)
ஏப்ளானோஸ்போர்க்கள் (p-57)
எப்பளானோஸ்போர்க்கள் (p-73)

சூல்முடி (p-58)
சூலகமுடி (p-59)

சூல்தண்டு (p-58)
சூலகதண்டு (p-59)

சூற்பை (p-58)
சூலகப்பை (p-59)

சூல்கள் (p-58)
சூலகம் (p-59)

குழல் உட்கரு (p-62)
குழாய் நியூகிளியஸ் (p-74)

பெபபோ (p-63)
பெபோ (p-64)
பெப்போ (p-65)

அன்னோனா ஸ்குவாமோசா (p-64)
அனோனா ஸ்கொயாமோசா (p-75)

சைக்கோனஸ் (p-64)
சைகோனஸ் (p-64)

கேரியாப்சிஸ் (p-64)
கார்யாப்சிஸ் (p-67)

கிரிமோகார்ப் (p-64)
க்ரெமோகார்ப் (p-67)

ட்ரைடாக்ஸ் (p-67)
டிரைடாக்ஸ் (p-71)

ஸ்கூட்டல்லம் (p-69)
ஸ்கூட்டெல்லம் (p-73)

ஏகைனீட்டுகள் (p-58)
ஏகைனெட்டுகள் (p-73)

Content of the unit 5

The fifth unit A Representative Study of Mammals contains the following chapters viz., Morphology, Habitats, Adaptations, Basic Physiological Functions, Circulatory System in man, Excretory system in man, Relationship of structure to functions, Animal Behavior and Some case studies from researchers.

Evidence of Criteria

From the above list of content it seemed that the contents are sufficient and appropriate for this age level of learners. They are sequenced in a logical order. Contents are presented according to maxims of learning such as know to unknown, easy to hard etc., In addition relation with real life experience and previous knowledge of learners was kept on presenting the concept. In this unit contains the clear idea about the functional and morphological adaptations of the mammals in relation to their habitats. But the conception given about the Circulatory system in man and Excretory system in man are not appropriate and also it was irrelevant to the topic. It has come under the unit VI Life process under the transportation of animals and excretion in animals vice versa.

Learning by doing was emphasized in this unit. The number activities provided in this unit are sufficient. These activities can be performed by utilizing locally available resources. The activities provided were relevant to the context. Opportunity of practical work was found in this unit. For example a practical work on measuring the rate of heart beat, measuring the body temperature etc., were found in this unit. Given verbal and writing exercises seemed to be not enough for this grade. It contains only the exercises like fill in the blanks and choosing the correct answer.

Illustrations areseemed to be appropriate and helpful for the learners understand the concepts easily and clearly. Necessary and adequate illustrations were found here. The size of the figures was appropriate and legible. For example LS of the human heart and the excretory system of man explained with clear and legible figures. In some cases, there was no description for illustration (p-84). In the figure 5.5 blood cells were given. But no description was found about the type of white blood cells such as Neutrophil, Monocyte, Lymphocyte, Eosinophil and Bosophil in the text.

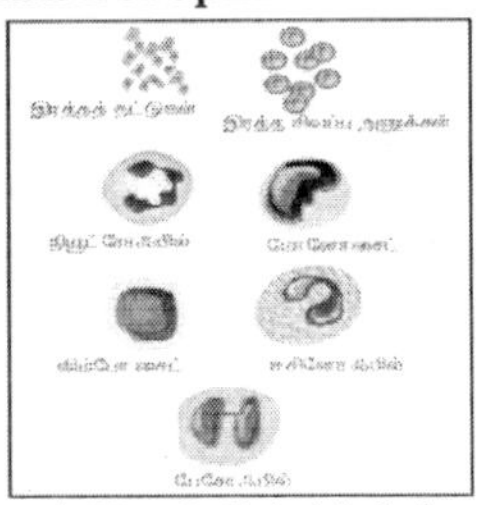

படம். 5.5 மனித இரத்தச் செல்கள்

Readability of the text seemed to be appropriate in this unit. Comprehensible vocabulary, easy and short length sentences were used in this unit. In some cases, uniformity in spelling is lacking.

ஆரிக்கிள்கள் (p-82)
ஆரிக்கில் (p-90)

வெண்ட்ரிகிள் (p-82)
வெண்ட்ரிக்கிள் (p-82)
வெண்ட்ரிக்கில் (p-90)

மேற்பெருஞ்சிறை (p-82)
மேல்பெரும்சிரை (p-82)

கீழ்பெரும்சிரை (p-82)
கீழ்பெருஞ்சிரை (p-82)

பிறை சந்திர வாழ்வு (p-82)
பிறை சந்திர வால்வு (p-82)

மிட்ரல் வாழ்வு (p-82)
மிட்ரல் வால்வு (p-82)

ஃபைபிரினோஜன் (p-84)
ஃபைபிரினோஜின் (p-90)

கார்ட்டெக்ஸ் (p-86)
கார்டெக்ஸ் (p-85)

கேப்சுல் (p-85)
கேப்சூல் (p-85)

ரீனல் பிரமீடு (p-86)
ரீனல் பிரமீடி (p-86)
ரீனல் பிரமிடு (p-85)

பேப்பில்லா (p-86)
பாப்பில்லா (p-86)

நெப்ரான் (p-86)
நெஃப்ரான்(p-86)

பெமனின் கிண்ணம் (p-86)
பெமானின் கிண்ணம் (p-86)

குளோமுருலஸ் (p-86)
குளோமருலஸ் (p-86)

Content of the Unit 6

The sixth unit Life Processes contains the following chapter's viz., Definition, Types of nutrition and human digestive system,

Respiration, Transportation in plants and animals, Nervous system, Co-ordination in plants, Movement due to growth and Hormones in animals.

Evidence of Criteria

From the above list of content it seemed that the contents are sufficient and appropriate for this age level of learners. They are sequenced in a logical order. Here the contents are presented in an attractive and interesting way. There was no prejudicial and controversial fact in this unit. Presented subject matters are adequate to build up scientific concept. Here the important life process like nutrition, respiration, transportation, excretion and coordination were described for lower level organisms to the higher order animals and also for the plants in a detailed manner. But the growth process was not mentioned for plants though it is an important life process. In this text only mentioned about the movement due to growth. The conception about the growth hormones is not given. The conception given in this unit such as types of nutrition, respiration and movements in plants all these topics were already discussed in the previous grade textbook (STD-IX, unit-IV, p-60). Here it was repeated again.

Learning by doing is emphasized in this unit. A lot of opportunity of practical work and exercises are found here. For example, in the chapter nutrition in plants, learners can perform the experiment on the chlorophyll is essential for photosynthesis. Then experiment on anaerobic respiration in plants, movement of water during transpiration in plants and phototropism in plants which will motivate the learners learning while doing. This unit is rich in verbal and writing exercises. These exercises included filling in the blanks, matching, choose the correct answer etc., especially found exercise within the text is really helpful for formative evaluation of learner's during reading the text.

Illustrations are seemed to be appropriate and helpful for the learners understand the concept easily and clearly. Necessary and adequate illustrations are given here. For example, the path of water across the root, and other life process were shown through easy and colorful illustrations.

Readability of the text seemed to be appropriate in this unit. Comprehensible vocabulary, easy and short length sentences were used in this unit. In some cases, uniformity in spelling is lacking.

மானோட்ரோபா (p-95)
மானோட்ரோப்பா (p-110)

மைட்டோகாண்ட்ரியா (p-97)
மைட்டோகோன்டிரியா (p-98)

ஆக்சிஜன் (p-98)
ஆக்ஸிஜன் (p-99)

கார்பன் டை ஆக்சைடு (p-98)
கார்பன் டை ஆக்ஸைடு (p-99)

ஃபுளோயம் (p-101, 102)
புளோயம் (p-101, 102)

டயாலைசிஸ் (p-104)
டயலேசிங் (p-105)

Content of the Unit 7

The seventh unit Conservation of Environment contains the following chapters viz., Bio degradable and non biodegradable wastes, Water management, Wild life Sanctuaries, Balance in Ecosystem, Coal and Petroleum, Green chemistry and Science today- Towards a global village.

Evidence of Criteria

From the above list of content it seemed that the contents are sufficient and appropriate for this age level of learners. They are sequenced in a logical order. They are found real life oriented also. Here, knowledge about fresh water management is real life oriented. It might help the learners developing their experimental and problem solving skill. And it is a suitable concept for this age group. Some concepts were almost whole repetition of what students learnt in previous grades. For example, water management and wildlife sanctuaries already given in the previous grade textbooks. Here it was repeated again. Some incorrect information was found in this unit. Here the type of ecosystem is mentioned as aquatic and terrestrial (p-

120). But the correct information is the type of ecosystem is Natural and Artificial. The conception provided in the chapter Balance in Ecosystem (p-110) is also given in the previous grade textbook under the unit Ecosystem (STD VII, unit 7, p-81). In the chapter coal and petroleum (p-114) the sources and effect of coal are given. But there is no conception about the control and alternate measures for coal pollution was found here. Lack of scientific concept and explanation were found in this chapter. For example no explanation was given about the impact of carbon-dioxide on global warming.

A little opportunity of practical work was found in this unit. Learning by doing was emphasized in this unit. The given activities can be performed by utilizing locally available resources. These activities are helping to develop the creativity of learner. For example, the activities like various ways to eliminate waste products, ways to reduce the use of coal and petroleum etc., motivate the learner's creativity and scientific temper. Provided verbal and writing exercise seemed to be enough for this grade. These exercises included filling in the blanks, choosing right answer, find the odd one out, freehand writing, drawing pictures etc., Exercise within the text was also present here.

Illustrations are seemed to be appropriate and helpful for the learners understand the concepts easily and clearly. Necessary and adequate illustrations are found here. For example, in this unit conservation of environment rain water harvesting (p-116) and domestic conservation method of water (p-117) are presented through easy and clear illustrations. In some cases, the size of the figure was inappropriate and also there was no description for illustration found in this unit. For example, food web (p-114) figure was given. But no description was found about it with the figure and also it was very complicated to understand by the learners.

படம் 7.7 உணவு வலை

Readability of the text seemed to be appropriate in this unit. Comprehensible vocabulary, easy and short length sentences were used in this unit. In some cases, uniformity in spelling is lacking.

கந்தகடை-ஆக்ஸைடு (p-113)
கந்தக-டை-ஆக்சைடு (p-128)

கார்போஹைடிரேட் (p-97)
கார்போஹைட்ரேட் (p-120)

ஹைட்ரஜன் (p-122)
ஹைடிரஜன் (p-127)

ஹைட்ரோ கார்பன்கள் (p-124)
ஹைடிரோ கார்பன்கள் (p-127)

ஹாலோஜன் (p-126)
ஹேலஜன் (p-127)

Content of the Unit 8

The eighth unit Waste Water Management contains the following chapters viz., Journey of water, Sewage, Treatment, Domestic practices, Sanitation and diseases, Alternate arrangement for sewage disposal, Sanitation in public places and Energy Management.

Evidence of Criteria

From the above list of content it seemed that the contents are sufficient and appropriate for this age level of learners. The contents are sequenced in a logical order. In addition relation with life experience and previous knowledge of learners was kept on presenting the concept. For example, further conception about the necessity of sewage water treatment and energy management was presented here relating to the idea given in the previous grade. Presented contents were relevant to the need of the society. The contents were real life oriented also. Here, knowledge about our role in energy conservation (p-140) is real life oriented. It might help the learners developing problem solving skills. And also it will motivate the learners to use the resources in a proper way.

Learning by doing was emphasized in this unit. The number activities provided in this unit were sufficient. These activities motivate the learners creative and scientific thinking to solve the problems. The activities provided are relevant to the context. A lot of opportunity for practical work and exercise are found here. For example, in the sewage water treatment learners will make the model for sewage water treatment by which they can learn the importance and method of wastewater treatment. Given verbal and writing exercises seemed to be not enough. The given exercises were logical level. It contains the exercises like choosing the correct answer, reasoning out, matching etc.,

Illustrations are seemed to be appropriate and helpful for the learners understand the concepts easily and clearly. Necessary and adequate illustrations were found here. For example, sewage water treatment (p-131) and production of solar energy (p-136) were presented through real life oriented attractive pictures.

Readability of the text seemed to be appropriate in this unit. Comprehensible vocabulary, easy and short length sentences were used in this unit. In some cases, uniformity in spelling is lacking.

புரோப்பேன் (p-137)
புரோபேன் (p-141)

ஈத்தேன் (p-137)
ஈதேன் (p-141)

பியூட்டேன் (p-138)
பியூடேன் (p-141)

Conceptual Errors

There are plenty of studies held in recent years focused on determination of alternative conceptions in science search and make compensation for their possible origins. It is mostly accepted that one of the main negative factors influencing pupils learning activity is the alternative conceptions. Alternative conceptions or misconceptions imply thinking patterns which do not mostly overlap with scientific realities (Bahar, 2003; Tekkaya, 2002). Since these thinking patterns developed by pupils mostly based on their own interpretations are contrary to scientific realities, they constitute a significant barrier against science education (Driver, 1989). It has been suggested that an alternative conception or misconception usually has three primary features given below. It is a cognitive idea that differs in a significant way from the scientific idea, it is held by a sizable proportion of the population, and it is notably resistant to being taught away; it is often described as a conceptual primitive (Clement, 1982). The studies have been shown that pupils usually develop alternative conceptions as a result of their own inter-pretations or from some contradictory explanations in school or out of school environments in early periods (Wandersee, Mintzes & Novak, 1994). Expressions of well known subjects by teachers or their expression in textbooks also may lead to alternative conceptions (Barrass, 1984; Sewell, 2002). Alternative conceptions are considerably widespread in formal education (Bishop & Anderson, 1990) and significantly resistant against change (Bahar, 2003; Wandersee et al., 1994). If they are not detected and compensated very early, they may continue for long years and may constitute significant barriers in understanding process. Some researchers have been detected that pupils have many alternative conceptions in biology in Turkey (Tekkaya, Çapa, & Yılmaz, 2000; Ascı, Özkan, & Tekkaya, 2001). In order to teach all pupils today's standards, teachers need to understand subject matter deeply and flexibly so they can help students create useful cognitive maps, relate one idea to another, and address alternative conception. Teachers need to see how ideas connect across fields and to everyday life. This kind of understanding may provide a foundation for pedagogical content knowledge that enables teachers to make ideas accessible to others (Shulman, 1986, 1987).

Oversimplification

"There are chloroplasts on cells in green color segments of plants. Simple sugar (glucose) and oxygen is provided by using water in the soil and carbon dioxide in the air in these organelles. This event is called as photosynthesis"
(p-93).

Photosynthesis

$$\text{Carbon dioxide + Water} \xrightarrow[\text{Chlorophyll}]{\text{Light}} \text{Glucose + Oxygen}$$

It is seen that photosynthesis activity is presented by oversimplifying with an equation. Hershey (2004) states that such types of simplifications made in texts in textbooks might lead to alternative conceptions in pupils. In the photosynthesis equation given here, simple sugar (glucose) is indicated as the main photosynthetic product. However, glucose is not a main photosynthetic product (Hershey, 2004). There is almost no free glucose generated in photosynthesis (Storey, 1989). The most general product generated in photosynthesis is starch and sucrose. Moreover, single arrow drawing in the photosynthesis equation incorrectly implies that photosynthesis occurs in one single stage. Multiple arrows should be used here (Hershey, 2004).

Under Generalizations

All organisms, except the green plants do not possess chloroplasts as they do not carry out photosynthesis (p-93). Chloroplasts do not only exist in green plants but also in photosynthetic protists in eukaryotic structure. For example, *Euglena* making photosynthesis has a chloroplast (Campbell & Reece, 2006).

Physical Aspects of the Textbook

Physical aspect of the book found strong. The title cover seemed to be really attracting. Printing pages in the textbook play a vital role of the textbook. Here, printing pages are clear, visible and legible for the students to read the textbook. The font, size and space between letters, words, sentences and paragraphs are matches the age of the learner. The tables and the charts given in the textbook provide the clearest picture of the contents. When the information's are given in the form of a table, diagram etc., it will reach effectively into the mind of the readers. Information in the text book is updated to the present scenario. The students using this textbook gain some new information to improve their knowledge. Good quality paper was used here. Binding and stitching was also sustainable. In some cases, the typographical error was found in this textbook. There was no printing mistake here. Overall the book was found sustainable and safe for the learner of this grade.

Some of the Common Errors Found in This Text

- The figures were not tied into the textual material by direct reference.
- In some cases, the topics and subtopics not organized with proper numbering.
- In some cases the important words are not given in the boldface.
- In each chapter the end summary was missing in this textbook.

- The scientific names of the organism have to be represented in italics it was missing in this textbook. But they gave it in the normal font.

Interpretations

- The content and language were relevant to the age level of the learners.
- The organization was not proper in some of the units (I, III, V, and VI).
- Illustrations seemed to be really attractive.
- Scope of formative and summative evaluation was found in this textbook.
- In addition, the book was found to be suitable for developing scientific skills among the learners. And developing scientific skills among the learners is the main objective of science education.
- The contents were also real life oriented and helpful for acquiring problem solving skills.
- The textbook serve fully to meet the needs of teachers, students and even instruction.
- The misconception and some incorrect information found in this textbook it should be rectified.
- Scientific research process, questioning, inquiry based instruction and problem solving skills are supported by the book.
- More writing exercises should be included in some units.
- Sufficient opportunity of practical work and creative work should be included.
- Relevant contents and activities should be included for attaining missing competencies.
- Correct information should be provided and less necessary information should be avoided.
- More scientific concepts should be included. Beside this relevant scientific explanation of scientific concepts should be provided.
- The number and diversity of examples should be increased.

SUGGESTIONS AND CONCLUSION

The content analysis made only with the 10th standard Science textbook. It has to be conducted all the standard science textbooks. The important skills in science study and the textbook should be studied vis-à-vis development of these skills in children.

The textbook is seen as the most popularly used teaching learning material. So the curriculum is to be transacted in the textbook in its full form. Since, the mostly used learning material in reality has been used by the teachers and students are textbook. So the textbook is the main instrument to acquire the pre-identified competencies. So it is worthwhile to evaluate the textbooks to examine how the curriculum has been presented in the textbooks and how much the textbooks are effective to transfer concepts, themes and processes into the learners intended for. In the light of the findings given above it seemed to be clear that the textbook should pay more attention to how we can draw ideas from learners and facilitate them to discover scientific concepts through experiments. So that learners should become scientifically literate. The findings and recommendation of the study might give guidelines to the textbook developers to take necessary steps to ensure the quality of science education for making the learner a scientifically literate person.

The content of the text is organized properly. Most of the matter presented in the textbook is accurate. The illustrations given in the textbook are appropriate. The material presented in the text is psychologically sound full. The learning activities presented in the text are appropriate and adequate.

REFERENCES

Sources: Books

1. Arumugam N. **A Text Book of Embryology,** Saras publication, 2005.
2. Best, John W. **Research in Education,** New Delhi: Prentice-Hall of India Private Limited, 1986.
3. Hemalatha Kalaimathi D. **Teaching of Biology,** New Delhi: Neelkamal publications Private Limited, 2010.
4. Kothari C.R, **Research Methodology**, New Age International (P) Ltd. Publication 2004.
5. Mariakuttikan A. **Animal Physiology,** Saras publication, 2007.
6. Saduh A.N, **Research Methodology in Social Sciences,** New Delhi Himalaya Publishing House, 1985.
7. Sharma R.N, **Research Methodology in Social Sciences,** Mumbai Media promoters & Publishers (P) Ltd, 1983.
8. Venugopal G. **Teaching of biology**, Chennai: Ram publishers, 2009.
9. Verma P.S. **Cytology,** S.Chand and Company Limited, 2006.

Sources: Journals

1. Abd-El-Khalick, (2008), "Representations of Nature of Science in High School Chemistry Textbooks over the Past Four Decades", Journal of
2. Research in Science Teaching, 45 (7), 835-855.
3. Ametller, J., & Pinto, R. (2002), "Students' Reading of Innovative Images of Energy at Secondary School Level", International Journal of Science Education, 24(3), 285-312.
4. Ahtineva, A. (2005), "Textbook Analysis in the Service of Chemistry Teaching", Universitas Scientiarum, 10(special issue), 25-33.
5. Bahar, M. (2003), "Misconceptions in Biology Education and Conceptual Change Strategies", Educational Sciences: Theory & Practice, 3(1), 55-64.
6. Barrass, R. (1984), "Some Misconceptions and Misunderstandings Perpetuated By Teachers and Textbooks of Biology", Journal of Biological Education, 18(3), 201-206.

7. Bazzul, (2011), "The Secret Identity of a Biology Textbook: Straight and Naturally Sexed", Cultural Studies of Science Education, 6 (2), 265-286
8. Bishop, B.A., & Anderson, C.W. (1990), "Student Conceptions of Natural Selection and Its Role in Evolution", Journal of Research in Science Teaching, 27(5), 415-427.
9. Clifford, P. (2002), "The Pressure-Flow Hypothesis of Phloem Transport: Misconceptions in the A-Level Textbooks", Journal of Biological Education, 36(3), 110-112.
10. Cook, M. (2008), "Students' Comprehension of Science Concepts Depicted in Textbook Illustrations", Electronic Journal of Science Education, 12(1), 1-14.
11. Delgato, Margaret H. (2009), "Considerations of Multicultural Science And Curriculum Reform: A Content Analysis of State-Adopted Biology Textbooks in Florida", ProQuest LLC, Ph.D. Dissertation, University of South Florida.
12. Dimopoulos, K., Koulaidis, V., & Sklaveniti, S. (2003), "Towards an Analysis of Visual Images in School Science Textbooks and Press Articles about Science and Technology" Research in Science Education, 33(2), 189-216.
13. Erdogan, (2009), "Components of Environmental Literacy in Elementary Science Education Curriculum in Bulgaria and Turkey", EURASIA Journal of Mathematics, Science & Technology Education, 5 (1), 15-26.
14. Eugene L. Chiappetta, (1993), "Do Middle School Life Science Textbooks Provide A Balance of Scientific Literacy Themes", Journal of Research in Science Teaching, 30 (7), 787-797.
15. Gericke, (2010), "Conceptual Variation in the Depiction of Gene Function in Upper Secondary School Textbooks", Science & Education, 19 (10), 963-994.
16. Gkitzia, (2011), "Development and Application of Suitable Criteria for the Evaluation of Chemical Representations in School Textbooks", Chemistry Education Research and Practice, 12 (1), 5-14.
17. Gonzalez-Rodriguez, (2009), "Plant Nutrition in Spanish Secondary Textbooks", Journal of Biological Education, 43 (4), 152-158.
18. Haggarty, L., & Pepin, B. (2002), "An Investigation of Mathematics Textbooks and Their Use in English, French And German Classrooms: Who Gets an Opportunity to Learn About", British Educational Research Journal, 28(4), 567-590.

19. Iztok Devetak,(2009), "States of Matter Explanations in Slovenian Textbooks for Students Aged 6 To 14", International Journal of Environmental & Science Education, 5 (2), 217-235.
20. Jose c. Otero, (1990), "Comprehension Evaluation and Regulation in Learning from Science Texts", Journal of Research in Science Teaching, 27 (5), 447-460.
21. Kahveci, (2010), "Quantitative Analysis of Science and Chemistry Textbooks for Indicators of Reform: A Complementary Perspective", International Journal of Science Education, 32 (11),1495-1519.
22. Kesidou, S., & Roseman, J. E. (2002), "How Well Do Middle School Science Programs Measure Up Findings From Project 2061's Curriculum Review", Journal of Research in Science Teaching, 39(6), 522-549.
23. Khalid Mahmood, (2009), "Textbook Evaluation through Quality Indicators: The Case of Pakistan", Bulletin of Education and Research, 31 (2), 1-27.
24. Levie, W. H., & Lentz, R. (1982), "Effects of Text Illustrations", Educational Communication and Technology, 30(4), 195-232.
25. Luli Stern, (2004), "Can Middle-School Science Textbooks Help Students Learn Important Ideas", Journal of Research in Science Teaching, 41 (6), 538-568.
26. Mandl, H., & Levin, J. R. (Eds.). (1989), "Knowledge Acquisition from Text and Pictures", Amsterdam: North-Holland.
27. Martínez-Gracia, M.V., Gil-Quílez, M.J., & Osada, J. (2006), "Analysis of Molecular Genetics Content in Spanish Secondary School Textbooks", Journal of Biological Education, 40(2), 35-60.
28. Michelle Cook, (2011), "Teachers' Use of Visual Representations in the Science Classroom", Science Education International, 22 (3), 175-184.
29. Miriam Lemmer, (2008), "Educators' Selection and Evaluation of Natural Science Textbooks", South African Journal of Education, 28, 175-187.
30. Musa Dikmenli, (2009), "Conceptual Problems in Biology-Related Topics in Primary Science and Technology Textbooks in Turkey", International Journal of Environmental & Science Education, 4 (4), 429-440.
31. Nakiboglu, (2011), "Analysis of Turkish High School Chemistry Textbooks and Teacher-Generated Questions about Gas Laws",

International Journal of Science and Mathematics Education, 9 (5), 1047-1071.

32. Norman G. Lederman, (1992), "Students' and Teachers' Conceptions of the Nature of Science", Journal of Research in Science Teaching, 29 (4), 331-359.
33. Peacock, A., & Gates, S. (2000), "Newly Qualified Primary Teachers' Perceptions of the Role of Text Material in Teaching Science", Research in Science & Technological Education, 18(2), 155-171.
34. Reid, D. J., Briggs, N., & Beveridge, M. (1983), "The Effect of Pictures upon the Readability of A School Science Topic", British Journal of Educational Psychology, 53(3), 327-335.
35. Rillero, Peter (2010), "The Rise and Fall of Science Education: A Content Analysis of Science in Elementary Reading Textbooks of the 19th Century", School Science and Mathematics, 110 (5), 277-286.
36. Schussler, (2010), "Exploring Plant and Animal Content in Elementary Science Textbooks", Journal of Biological Education, 44 (3), 123-128.
37. Shulman, L.S. (1987), "Knowledge and Teaching: Foundations of the New Reform" Harvard Educational Review, 57(1), 1-22.
38. Slough, Scott W. (2010), "Science Textbooks' Use of Graphical Representation: A Descriptive Analysis of Four Sixth Grade Science Texts", Reading Psychology, 31 (3), 301-325.
39. Storey, R.D. (1992), "Textbook Errors and Misconceptions in Biology: Cell Energetic", The American Biology Teacher, 54(3), 161-166.
40. Vasilis Koulaidis, (1996), "A Pedagogical Analysis of Science Textbooks", Research in Science Education, 26(1), 55-71.

Sources: Internet

1. http://www.asian-efl-journal.com/Litz_thesis.pdf
2. http://writing.colostate.edu/guides/research/content/com2b1.cfm
3. www.project2061.org/publications/**textbook**/mgsci/.../**analysis**.hm
4. www.questia.com/.../**book/content-analysis**-for-the-social-**sciences**-and-humanities-by-ole-r-holsti.jsp
5. http://www.ischool.utexas.edu/~palmquis/courses/content.html
6. www.google.com
7. www.eric.ed.gov
8. www.springerlink.com
9. www.**samacheerkalvi**.in
10. www.textbooksonline.tn.nic.in
11. www.**ncert**.nic.in
12. www.ncert.nic.in/rightside/links/pdf/**framework**/prelims.pdf